100 and More Ways not to be a Gangster but have your American Dream

100 and More Ways not to be a Gangster but have your American Dream

John Adeagbo

Library of Congress Control Number: 2010900232
ISBN: Softcover   978-1-4500-2378-8

To order additional copies of this book, contact:
Xlibris Corporation
1-888-795-4274
www.Xlibris.com
Orders@Xlibris.com
72341

Dedication

I want to dedicate this book to Karen Harshaw who inspired me and help me stay in this great country. My daughter Kianna and son Jai Scott. Amanda Lara who encourage me to write this book. Also, I want to thank everybody from the bottom of my heart who made it possible to complete this book Shannon Tyler, Julia Rivas, Dennis Gyrad. I hope am able to help one person I have done my job. If that is the case I'm satisfied. Also, thank you to the one above. Thank you, Thank you!

INTRODUCTION

THIS IS AN inspiration or self help book for immigrant, citizens, foreigners and everybody to live the American dream to their full potential.

This is a book for our children because they are the future. After reading this book their life would never be the same again.

It is the book that will help you make it or break you in this country. It is for everybody who wants to be somebody. It gives you the life experience not to be a gangster but live your American dream.

I have sought you with all my heart, don't let me wander from your commands.

Psalms 119.9-11

1. If you don't know traveling is part of education. The more you travel to different places. The more knowledge you have. If not you are wasting time and money.

2. If you don't want to get married always make sure you have your family, friends, there for you. If not, you will be wasting time and money.

3. If you don't cook and eat out all the time. Once in a while (blue moon) you are wasting time and money.

4. If you don't change your habits you will get the same results. But if you change your habits ways you get a different result. If not you will be wasting time and money.

5. If you don't know what to do as a teenager between (18-25) years and looking for a career you can always joined the military, navy, marine great benefits. You can always use it as a foundation to run for public office. If not you are wasting time and money.

6. If you don't depend on yourself and have faith in God, you will be disappointed, if you depend on people. People are human and are not perfect. If not you are wasting time and money.

7. If you don't stay in marriage but have children with different men or fathers because of peer pressure you will be wasting time and money.

8. If you don't practice safe sex until you ready to have a family you will be raising children by yourself instead of you finishing school. Again, you be wasting time and money.

9. If you don't pray daily, and meditate you will end up in problems e.g. Christians, Muslims, Catholics, etc. If not you will be wasting time and money.

10. If you don't know it is easy to get into trouble but difficult to get out. If not you will be wasting time and money.

11. If you don't filed and pay taxes it would be difficult getting your citizenship (foreigners.) If not you will be wasting time and money.

12. If you don't plan ahead of time you will be wasting time and money.

13. If you don't stay focus and you go to parties all the time you will be wasting time and money.

14. If you don't know how to be a parent you must borrow ideas from other parents whose children have turn out great. If not you will be wasting time and money.

15. If you don't know how to stay in marriage, see a counselor and ask other couples how they did it for so many years. If not you will be wasting time and money.

16. If you don't stay in marriage you will not get great benefits like refund on taxes, cheaper health care etc. Again, you will be wasting time and money.

17. If you don't save money when young and wait until you get old you will be wasting time and money.

18. If you don't like university or college make sure you have a skill, go to a trade school for mechanic, plumber, carpenter, etc. If not you will be wasting time and money.

19. If you don't buy American cars because is easy to maintain and parts are cheaper and anybody can work on the car. You will be wasting time and money on foreign cars with high maintenance (b-m-w, Mercedes, Saab, etc).

20. If you don't know where to get expensive parts on your car you can always go to the junkyard motor parts are from new vehicles involved in accident. If not you will be wasting time and money.

21. If you don't know what to do with your life and you are a teenager (16-24) age. You can join the job corp. You received hands on career training in any field. This program is funded by the govt. If not you will be wasting your time and money.

22. If don't take care of your children they would not be there for you. Again be there for them so they can be there for you. If not you will be wasting time and money.

23. If you don't teach your children to speak a second language (bilingual) you limit their opportunities. We live in a global world. Again, you be wasting time and money.

24. If you don't obey the traffic laws you over speed and drink, your license will be revoked, it will be hard getting a good paying position, and most jobs required transportation. Again, driving is a priviledge not a license to kill. If not you be wasting time and money.

25. If you don't stay in marriage before you have children. The children don't really get to know you. Children are supposed to be there for you, you for them. If not you end up with child support, until eighteen years old by then it is too late. Again, wasting time and money. As the saying goes two eyes are better than one eye.

26. If you don't filed and pay taxes on time you get penalized paying interest rates and late fee. Again, wasting time and money.

27. If you don't belong to any religious organizations like church, mosque, temple, Buddhist, etc. You will be wasting time and money. As the saying goes information is power. Also is a good place for network and information.

28. If you don't have any associations, sororities, organizations that you are a member joined one and network , make you stay out of trouble . If not you will be wasting time and money.

29. If you don't get your green card, citizenship, permit resident as a foreigner in the United States. You have no rights to benefits, unemployment, financial aid, could face deportation anytime. You have no voice get your papers. If not you be wasting time and money.

30. If you don't keep a good credit score. You cannot get apartment, house, loan, car, good paying job. Your life is based on your credit. Again, you will be wasting time and money.

31. If you don't have papers for foreigners it would be difficult to achieve your American dream get reliable govt jobs, owning business. Again, you be wasting time and money.

32. If you don't dress well at all times (first impression last impression). It will cost you jobs and opportunities. Again, you be wasting time and money. Boys, (pants hanging down your legs) and girls showing you know what?

33. If you don't buy furniture, clothes from thrift stores low budget stores, Wal-Mart, Kmart, it will cost you lots of money. Some of the furniture, clothes in the thrift store are new. These are rich people giving donations to charities. Again, if not you will be wasting time and money.

34. If you don't cook natural foods but eat all the time fast food. This will result to high cholesterol, overweight, high blood pressure, diabetes. Again wasting time and money.

35. If you don't get advice from a mentor, or somebody doing better than you. For example, father, pastor, teacher, people might be reluctant to help you. Misery like company or should I say may be they can not handle your progress. Again, don't waste your time and money.

36. If you don't accomplished your dream you might get discourage by people and killed your dreams. Again, you wasting time and money.

37. If you don't speak a second language, bilingual, French, Spanish, German, African, Russian. You limit yourself the world is global. The more languages you speak the more opportunities you have over a person who speak one language. Again, don't waste time and money.

38. If you don't buy things with cash you will end up with high interest rates, bad credit, late fees. Always use credit card for emergencies. Again, not wasting time and money.

39. If you don't have a time limit for odd jobs/ any jobs with no benefits, insurance, promotion. Sometimes you get addicted to the quick money while you could have gone to a trade school or college one or two years learned a skill or trade. Again, don't waste your time and money plan for your future.

40. If you don't understand the system, learn the system it is man made or it will be hard for you to come back when you make mistakes. Work the system to your advantage. If not you will be wasting time and money.

41. If you don't solve your problems immediately quickly it would be out of control. Again, you wasting time and money.

42. If you don't have a good paying position, don't buy a new car because it can lead to high notes, bad credit, if you lost your job. A car is not an investment is a necessity. Again, don't waste your time and money.

43. If you don't exercise or have a hobby you love doing running, biking, and gymnastics. There is consequences health problems, high blood pressure, diabetes, stroke, cancer. As the saying goes health is wealth. If not you will be wasting time and money.

44. If you don't eat right there is also consequences health problems, high blood pressure, diabetes, stroke. Eat right and stay healthy fruits, vegetable, salad. If not you will be wasting time and money.

45. If you don't do check ups there is consequences make sure you see the doctor regularly. The saying goes prevention is always better than cure. If not, you be wasting time and money.

46. If you don't obey the laws, very important. Your life change forever you can't find a good paying job because of your past, most likely you go back doing something illegal and back in jail. Again, you wasting your time and money.

47. If you don't obey the laws and you are doing illegal activities like drugs, prostitution (because everyone does it does not make it right). Finish school instead of you going for the quick money. (You don't stay young forever, or nothing lasts forever). Again go to school don't waste your time and money.

48. If you don't try to be a leader instead of a follower you will end up in trouble. Most leaders are thinkers while followers are like everyone else. Be yourself; don't waste your time and money.

49. If you don't take control of your life somebody else will control your life. Again, don't waste your time and money. Have self control of your life.

50. If you don't teach your children your history, heritage, culture they would be lost and confused. Teach them your history so they are ready for the future. If not you will be wasting time and money.

51. If you don't get married it would be difficult making it in the big cities. Unless you have a high paying position. If not you will be wasting time and money.

52. If you don't know how to speak or communicate. Your chances of getting a good paying job is limited. Don't limit yourself learn to speak properly or you will be wasting time and money.

53. If you don't practice safe sex but have unprotected sex until you are ready to have children you will be raising a family by yourself, paying child support. Again, don't waste your time and money.

54. If you don't protect yourself or practice safe sex you might catch all types of diseases, HIV, herpes, gonorrhea, etc. If not you wasting time and money.

55. If you don't have a job and looking for a job look for one with group insurance and benefits no underwriting everyone is covered. If not you get sick or injured no coverage. Again, you are wasting time and money.

56. If you don't have a job you can always go on line to apply for jobs. Send and attached your resume e.g. website, *www.master.com, www.joboptions, www. careermosaic.com.* If not you will be wasting time and money.

57. If you don't have insurance make sure you plan for your future before you get old. (Final expenses). If not you will be wasting time and money.

58. If you don't have investments like pension, 401k, life insurance, annuities before you retired or old. Again, it will cost you time and money.

59. If you don't have any insurance e.g. life insurance it will cost you. Parent you want your children to do better than you so plan for their future and yourself. If not you will be wasting time and money.

60. If you don't get insurance while young or healthy, it will cost you high premiums, deductibles when you get old. Again, wasting time and money.

61. If you don't get insurance coverage while you young healthy. It would be late getting it when you are ill and sick. Again, you wasting time and money.

62. If you don't have a plan always have options plan A and B. If not you will be wasting time and money

63. If you don't have a goal and deadline where you see yourself in three to five years your life and goals would be incomplete. Again, don't waste your time and money. Achieve your goal!

64. If you don't upgrade your resume and follow up quickly on jobs you will be unemployed. Again, wasting time.

65. If you don't want to do the time don't commit the crime. If not you will be wasting time and money.

66. If you don't raised your children in the suburbia or country more likely they will end up in trouble in the cities. As the saying goes prevention is better than cure they get hook to the fast lane. Again, wasting time and money.

67. If you don't have savings you would not make it when there is surprise/ or emergencies. Always put money aside for the raining day. Again, if not it will cost you time and money.

68. If you don't pay your rent with your first week pay check. You will be struggling trying to pay up or catch up. Again, don't waste your time and money.

69. If you don't spend some money for x-mass live everyday like x-mass day. If not you will be wasting time and money.

70. If you don't know the laws and sentences in different states before you commit a crime don't commit the crime. E.g. armed robbery, drugs, crack, heroine, shoplifting this are felonies. Again, don't waste your time and money.

71. If you don't do things independently like, cutting your hair, lawn, doing your laundry, oil change, manicure. You will be wasting time and money.

72. If you don't know how to drive you can always go to a driving school. Most positions required you to have a license (license to success). If not you will be wasting time and money.

73. If you don't drive American cars (ford, Chevy, etc), because it is easy maintenance but drive foreign cars (Mercedes, bmw, jaguar) high maintenance you will be wasting time and money.

74. If you don't teach your children to be financial responsible they will end up broke with bad credit. Again, wasting time and money.

75. If you don't have balance in your life physically (Be in shape, take care of your health). Spiritually, (church, mosque, Buddhist, Hindu, catholic). .Financially, (investments, annuities, insurance, pension, mutual funds). You will be lost. Again, you will be wasting time and money.

76. If you don't buy a small house you can afford but try to keep up with the Jones by buying a big house. It will cost you high mortgage and interest rates. Again, wasting time and money.

77. If you don't learn from your mistake you will make it a pattern (habit) and repeat them. But if you do learn from your mistakes and turn it positive. Again, you are not wasting time and money.

78. If you don't have a new car and the parts are expensive. There is always the junkyard some of the parts are from new vehicle involved in accident. The parts are cheap and it would save you time and money.

79. If you don't know where to get a car because of high car note go to the auction. The vehicles are cheaper and you know what is wrong with the vehicle. If not you will be wasting time and money.

80. If you don't work smart you will work harder. Use your head not your strength or should I say work smarter not harder. So you don't waste time and money.

81. If you don't belong to a church, mosque, temple, etc. You can always joined one and network with other members. This will keep you from been idle. If not you will be wasting time and money.

82. If you don't know how to use computer. Go to class / school and learn how to use it. Most positions are computer related. If not you will be wasting time and money. This is a must skill (do or die).

83. If you don't go to school and study what you love doing. You will not be happy. For example, entertainment, we all like to be entertained, singing, sport, acting. If not you will be wasting time and money.

84. If you don't invest while young and healthy it will end up costing you more money when you old not healthy and retired so plan for the future. If not you will be wasting time and money

85. If you don't have a job or a less paying job you can always learn new skills/ trade to make more money. If not you will be wasting time and money.

86. If you don't upgrade your resume it would be difficult finding the type of job you like. If not you will be wasting time and money.

87. If you don't want to go to school in the city. You can go to school in the country. It is easy to be focus and complete your goals. If not you will be wasting time and money. After you finished your goals you can come back to the city (trouble free) get that high paying position.

88. If you don't follow your dream different cities and states are known for different skills. Actors, (California) singers, (NY, CA) politics (dc) oil (Houston, Alaska). Finances (NY). Las Vegas (show business/ casino). If not you will be wasting time and money.

89. If you don't look for a career or profession/ skills that is needed all over the world e.g. mechanic most people drive vehicles, (science) doctor, nurses everybody would get sick one day, etc. If not you will be wasting time and money.

90. If you don't bank with a credit union where interest rates are not too high and is easy to get loans. If not you will be wasting time and money.

91.If you don't like the private industry you can always work for the govt, fed, local, or be a law enforcement officer. They have great benefits than the private industry and is more secured. If not you will be wasting time and money.

92. If you don't get married with the same religious background and culture. There is always exception to the rule. If not you will be wasting time and money.

93. If you don't speak and communicate to your child lead by example. And tell them the problems and consequences out there if not it will be too late. You will be wasting time and money.

94. If you don't plan for the future for your children they would have to do it the hard way. Why not make it easy and cheaper by planning ahead. If not you will be wasting time and money.

95. If you don't do laundry instead of dry cleaning your clothes it will cost you time and money.

96. If you don't have a mentor (a person you look up to for advice) pastor, rabbi, father, mother, you can always hired a coach somebody who will motivate you. So you achieved your goals. If not you will waste time and money.

97. If you don't write ideas (plans) on paper you will forget. It will cost you time and money. Because what you conceived is what you achieved. If not you are wasting time and money.

98. If you don't know the laws (politics) in different states (republican states) and (democratic states) conservative states and liberal states before moving there it will cost you. Again wasting time and money.

99. If you don't like a city, county, state, it might not be right place for your talent. You can always relocate to another state, city, county with different opportunities. If not you will be wasting time and money.

100. If you don't have a job and you are unemployed you can always go to temp agencies (manpower, labor ready etc). Some are weekly pay, daily pay, until you get a job. If not you will be wasting time and money.

101. If you don't obey the laws and know the laws in most states before relocating it will cost you time and money. Be a law abiding citizen and know your rights.

102. If you don't have a (high) credit score. It will cost you. Always check with credit companies about your credit. (Your life is based on your credit. if you don't have credit you can always establish your credit. If not you will be wasting time and money.

103. If you don't know how to listen, understand before you talk you will be wasting time and money.

104. If you don't have a plan always have plan A and B. if not you will be wasting time and money.

105. If you don't stand for something you stand for anything. Again, don't waste your time and money.

106. If don't have a budget that equals your income you will be wasting time and money.

107. If you don't plan for your needs (rent, food, transportation, phone) instead of your wants (clothes, shoes, parties, clubbing). Again,you will be wasting time and money.)

108. If you don't have financial goals and have a commitment to reach your goals. You will be wasting time and money.

109. If you don't do something you never done or get something you never had. Again, you will be wasting time and money.

110. If you don't plant seeds and harvest later you will be wasting time and money.

111. If you don't surround yourself with people smarter than you instead with people dumber than you. It starts rubbing of you. Again, you don't need that you be wasting time and money.

112. If you don't identify your dream and find company of people who do what you do (again, you be wasting time and money.

113. If you don't have a job you can start your own business something you love doing. If not you be wasting time and money.

114. If you don't managed your time wisely more time to important things. Again, if not you will be wasting time and money.

115. If you don't challenged yourself what are you living for. If not you will be wasting time and money.

116. If you don't have a vision for the future your future is going to be a repeat of the past, if not you will be wasting time and money.

117. If you don't teach your children to find solutions in life. They will be lost. Again, wasting time and money.

118. If you don't have a personal doctor, attorney, bondsman when you in trouble or get sick. Again you will be wasting time and money.

119. If you don't control your anger and you involved in domestic violence. You will be wasting time and money.

120. If you don't think positively (hope, desire, faith, love) but negatively (fear, anger, jealousy, hatred)etc. Again, you will be wasting time and money.

PROFILE:

JOHN ADEAGBO, (JD) as I'm call by most of my friends is a resident of Washington D.C (Nations Capital) for the past twenty nine years. I was born in the United Kingdom, Great Britain came to the United States as a teenager (nineteen years old) to finish my education. First, I went to Strayer college, Washington, D.C. Then, later on to the University of the District of Columbia, Washington. D.C. I'm a father of two children, Kianna and Jai with brothers, nephews, nieces, cousins, uncles scattered all over the World from Europe, North America to Africa. One of my hobbies or passion should I say is writing and trying to make the World a better place for us. This is one way I think I could bridge the gap between us so one can fulfilled their American dream. Presently I'm a business owner and a certified Producer for life and health insurance in the Nations Capital, Washington, D.C.